SELECTED POEMS

Robert Burns

I

CANONGATE POCKET CLASSICS

First published as a Pocket Classic in 2001 by
Canongate Books Ltd, 14 High Street, Edinburgh
EH1 1TE.

10 9 8 7 6 5 4 3 2 1

The publishers gratefully acknowledge general
subsidy from the Scottish Arts Council towards
the Canongate Classics and Pocket Classics series.

Typeset in 10pt Plantin by Hewer Text Ltd,
Edinburgh.

Printed and bound by Omnia Books, Glasgow.

British Library Cataloguing-in-Publication Data
A catalogue record for this volume
is available on request from the
British Library.

ISBN 1 84195 155 2

www.canongate.net

SELECTED POEMS

ROBERT BURNS

Robert Burns (1759–96) entered the world on 25 January as the first of William Burnes and Agnes Brown's seven children (four boys and three girls). Burnes was not a successful farmer and had to struggle with harsh land and demanding factors first at Mount Oliphant and then at Lochlie farm at Tarbolton. Nevertheless, he aimed to give Robert and his brother Gilbert a decent education, sending them to village schools and making arrangements for Robert to spend some of the summer months studying French and Mathematics with his former teacher as tutor. By the age of 15 Burns was widely read in English literature and considered something of a 'prodigy' in French, but it seems likely that hard labour on the farm weakened his heart and eventually contributed to an early death.

Forming a Bachelors' club and debating society at Tarbolton, young Robert became a Freemason, worked as a flax dresser in Irvine and enjoyed an active social and sexual life. He began to write poems, inspired to use Scots by the work of Robert Fergusson. His father's illness, his debts, and a court case over his rent arrears brought the poet back to Lochlie and when William Burnes died in 1784, Robert and Gilbert took up a farm at nearby Mossgiel and found themselves supporting the family. By this time Burns was involved with Betty Paton, by whom he had a daughter, and Jean Armour was also pregnant. (She was to bear him two pairs of twins before he eventually married her in 1788.) During these years (1784–6) Burns wrote some his most famous poems, including many epistles to various friends, his attacks on religious hypocrisy 'Holy Willie's Prayer', his celebration of Rabelaisian energy in 'The Holy Fair' and 'The Jolly Beggars' and his subtle but scathing satire on social injustice 'The Twa Dogs'. Creative or not, these were difficult and exhausting years and faced with local scandal, nervous strain, unrewarding hard labour and rising debt, Burns considered emigrating to Jamaica. The success of his first collection, *Poems, Chiefly in the Scottish Dialect* (1786) did much to change his mind. This first 'Kilmarnock Edition' sold out and a revised 'Edinburgh Edition' followed in 1787 to even greater acclaim, with an American edition published the following year.

Burns spent the winters of 1786–7 and 1787–8 in Edinburgh, lionised by society and the literary establishment, if largely misunderstood and sentimentalised by them as a 'heaven-taught ploughman'. Despite his literary success, however, Burns found it difficult to get any money from his Edinburgh publisher, William Creech, and was still in need of a patron or a job. Having spent the summer months of these years touring the Borders and the Highlands, he took an interest in old Scots songs and this led to his writing, collecting and rewriting songs for Johnson's *Scots Musical Museum* (1787–1803) and *Thomson's Select Scottish Airs* (1793–1818), a major task to which he devoted himself for the rest of his life. The poet took up farming again at Ellisland in the summer of 1788, and set about training to be an Excise Officer. The farm at Ellisland was not a success, and in 1791 Burns moved to Dumfries where he took up the post of Excise Officer. These last years were times of considerable political and social unrest throughout Britain and in 1795 severe shortages and food riots broke out in Dumfries. Burns's health was as uncertain as his finances. The poet's weak heart was exacerbated by the medicines of the day and, fevered and fearing for the future of his family, he died at home on 21 July 1796 at the age of 37.

Contents

The Twa Dogs: A Tale   1

To a Louse   13

To a Mouse   17

Address to the Deil   21

Address to a Haggis   29

Holy Willie's Prayer   33

Tam o' Shanter: A Tale   39

A Man's a Man for a' That   51

Such a Parcel of Rogues in a Nation   53

Westlin Winds   55

A Red, Red Rose   57

Mary Morison   59

Ae Fond Kiss   61

Auld Lang Syne   63

The Twa Dogs: A Tale

'Twas in that place o' *Scotland's* isle
That bears the name of auld King COIL,   old, Kyle
Upon a bonie day in June,   bonny
When wearing thro' the afternoon,
Twa Dogs, that were na thrang at hame,   two, not busy, home
Forgather'd ance upon a time.   met by chance, once

The first I'll name, they ca'd him *Caesar*,   called
Was keepet for his Honor's pleasure: kept
His hair, his size, his mouth, his lugs,   ears
Shew'd he was nane o' Scotland's dogs;   none
But whalpet some place far abroad,   pupped
Whare sailors gang to fish for Cod.   where, go

His locked, letter'd, braw brass-collar
Shew'd him the *gentleman* an' *scholar*;
But tho' he was o' high degree,
The fient a pride, na pride had he;   fiend, no
But wad hae spent an hour caressan,   would have

I

Ev'n wi' a Tinkler-gipsey's *messan*;   mongrel
At *Kirk* or *Market*, *Mill* or *Smiddie*,   smithy
Nae tawtied *tyke*, tho' e'er sae duddie,   matted cur, so ragged
But he wad stan't, as glad to see him,   would have stood
An' stroan't on stanes an' hillocks wi' him.   pissed, stones

The tither was a *ploughman's collie*,
A rhyming, ranting, raving billie,   fellow/ character
Wha for his friend an' comrade had him,   who
And in his freaks had *Luath* ca'd him,
After some dog in *Highland Sang*,
Was made lang syne, Lord knows how lang.   long ago

He was a gash an' faithfu' *tyke*,   wise, dog
As ever lap a sheugh or dyke!   leapt, ditch, stone wall
His honest, sonsie, baws'nt face   friendly, white marks
Ay gat him friends in ilka place;   always got, every
His *breast* was white, his touzie *back*   shaggy
Weel clad wi' coat o' glossy black;   well covered
His gawsie tail, wi' upward curl,   fine/full
Hung owre his hurdies wi' a swirl.   over, buttocks

Nae doubt but they were fain o' ither,   no, fond of each other
And unco pack an' thick thegither;   kept secrets/ confidential
Wi' social *nose* whyles snuff'd an' snowcket;   whiles, sniffed

Whyles mice an' moudiewurks they howcket; *whiles, moles, dug for*

Whyles scour'd awa' in lang excursion, *whiles, long*

An' worry'd ither in *diversion*;

Till tir'd at last wi' monie a farce, *many*

They sat them down upon their arse,

An' there began a lang digression *long*

About the *lords o' the creation*.

CAESAR

I've aften wonder'd, honest *Luath*, *often*

What sort o' life poor dogs like you have;

An' when the *gentry's* life I saw,

What way poor bodies liv'd ava. *at all*

Our *Laird* gets in his racked rents, *extortionate payments in kind, dues*

His coals, his kane, an' a' his stents:

He rises when he likes himsel;

His flunkies answer at the bell; *servants*

He ca's his coach; he ca's his horse; *calls*

He draws a bonie, silken purse, *carries*

As lang's my *tail*, whare thro' the steeks, *long as, where, stiches*

The yellow, letter'd *Geordie* keeks. *guinea (King's head) peeps*

Frae morn to een it's nought but toiling, *from, evening, nothing*

At baking, roasting, frying, boiling;

An' tho' the gentry first are steghan, *cramming*

Yet ev'n the *ha' folk* fill their peghan *hall (servants), stomach*

Wi' sauce, ragouts, an sic like trashtrie, *such like, rubbish*

That's little short o' downright wastrie: *wastage*

Our *Whipper-in*, wee, blastit wonner, *small, blasted wonder*

Poor, worthless elf, it eats a dinner,

Better than onie *Tenant-man* *any*

His Honor has in a' the lan': *all the land*

An' what poor *Cot-folk* pit their painch in, *put, paunch*

I own it's past my comprehension.

LUATH

Trowth, *Caesar*, whyles they're fash'd eneugh: *sometimes, bothered*

A *Cotter* howckan in a sheugh, *farm labourer, digging, ditch*

Wi' dirty stanes biggan a dyke, *stones, building, stone wall*

Bairan a quarry, an' sic like, *clearing, such*

Himsel, a wife, he thus sustains,

A smytrie o' wee duddie weans, *number, small ragged children*

An' nought but his han'-daurk, to keep *hands' work*

Them right an' tight in *thack an' raep*. *snug, thatch, rope*

An' when they meet wi' sair disasters, *sore*

Like loss o' health or want o' masters,

Ye maist wad think, a wee touch langer,

An' they maun starve o' cauld and hunger:

But how it comes, I never kend yet,

They're maistly wonderfu' contented;

An' buirdly chiels, an' clever hizzies,

Are bred in sic a way as this is.

most would,
longer

should, cold

knew

mostly
stout lads,
girls

such

CAESAR

But then to see how ye're neglecket,

How huff'd, an' cuff'd, an' disrespecket!

Lord man, our gentry care as little

For *delvers*, *ditchers*, an' sic cattle;

They gang as saucy by poor folk,

As I wad by a stinkan brock.

neglected

scolded, slapped,
disrespected

labourers,
diggers, such

go, smugly
would,
badger

I've notic'd, on our Laird's *court-day*,

(An' monie a time my heart's been wae),

Poor tenant bodies, scant o' cash,

How they maun thole a *Factor's* snash:

He'll stamp an' threaten, curse an' swear

He'll *apprehend* them, *poind* their gear;

While they maun staun', wi' aspect humble,

An' hear it a', an' fear an' tremble!

many, sad
short of
money
would suffer,
abuse

seize & sell
their goods

must stand

all

I see how folk live that hae riches;   have
But surely poor-folk maun be wretches!   must

LUATH

They're nae sae wretched's ane wad think: not so, as one would
Tho' constantly on poortith's brink,   poverty's
They're sae accustom'd wi' the sight,   so
The view o't gies them little fright.   gives

Then chance an' fortune are sae guided,   so
They're ay in less or mair provided;   always, more
An' tho' fatigu'd wi' close employment,
A blink o' rest's a sweet enjoyment.

The dearest comfort o' their lives,
Their grushie weans an' faithfu' wives;   thriving children
The *prattling things* are just their pride,
That sweetens a' their fire-side.

An' whyles twalpennie worth o' *nappy*   sometimes, ale
Can mak the bodies unco happy: folk, very
They lay aside their private cares,
To mind the Kirk an' State affairs;
They'll talk o' *patronage* an' *priests*,
Wi' kindling fury i' their breasts,

Or tell what new taxation's comin,
An' ferlie at the folk in Lon'on.

wonder

As bleak-fac'd Hallowmass returns,
They get the jovial, rantan *Kirns*,
When *rural life*, of ev'ry station,
Unite in common recreation;
Love blinks, Wit slaps, an' social Mirth
Forgets there's *Care* upo' the earth.

*festival of
All-Saints
harvest
homes*

That *merry day* the year begins,
They bar the door on frosty win's;
The nappy reeks wi' mantling ream,
An' sheds a heart-inspiring steam;
The luntan pipe, an' sneeshin mill,
Are handed round wi' right guid will;
The cantie, auld folks, crackan crouse,
The young anes rantan thro' the house —
My heart has been sae fain to see them,
That I for joy hae *barket* wi' them.

winds

*ale, foaming
froth*

*smoking,
snuff box*

*good
jolly old, chatting,
cheerful
ones,
running*

so content

have barked

Still it's owre true that ye hae said
Sic game is now owre aften play'd;
There's monie a creditable *stock*
O' decent, honest, fawsont folk,

*over, have
such a, over
often*

many

respectable

Are riven out baith root an' branch,   thrown out by
                                                        force, both
Some rascal's pridefu' greed to quench,

Wha thinks to knit himsel the faster   who

In favor wi' some *gentle Master*,

Wha, aiblins thrang a *parliamentin'*,   who, maybe
                                                        crowd
For *Britain's guid* his saul indentin' –   good, soul
                                                        engaged

CAESAR

Haith, lad, ye little ken about it: an exclamation,
                                                        know
For Britain's guid! guid faith! I doubt it.   good

Say rather, gaun as PREMIERS lead him: go

An' saying *aye* or *no's* they bid him:

At Operas an' Plays parading,

Mortgaging, gambling, masquerading:

Or maybe, in a frolic daft,

To HAGUE or CALAIS takes a waft,

To mak *a tour* an' tak a whirl,

To learn *bon ton*, an' see the worl'.   Fr. good
                                                        breeding

There, at VIENNA or VERSAILLES,

He rives his father's auld entails;   splits, old

Or by MADRID he taks the rout,   road
To thrum guittarres an' fecht wi' *nowt*;   strum guitars,
                                                        fight with bulls
Or down *Italian Vista* startles,   courses

Whore-hunting amang groves o' myrtles: among

Then bowses drumlie *German-water*,   drinks
                                           muddy
To mak himsel look fair an' fatter,

An' clear the consequential sorrows,

Love-gifts of Carnival Signioras.

For Britain's guid! for her destruction!

Wi' dissipation, feud an' faction!

LUATH

Hech man! dear sirs! is that the gate   way

They waste sae monie a braw estate!   so many

Are we sae foughten an' harass'd   so troubled

For gear ta gang that gate at last!   wealth to go

O would they stay aback frae courts,   away from

An' please themsels wi' countra sports,   country

It wad for ev'ry ane be better,   would,
                                           every one
The *Laird*, the *Tenant*, an' the *Cotter*!

For thae frank, rantan, ramblan billies,   they,
                                           fellows
Fient haet o' them's ill-hearted fellows; few of them
                                           are
Except for breakin o' their timmer,   timber

Or speakin lightly o' their *limmer*,   mistress

Or shootin of a hare or moor-cock,

The ne'er-a-bit they're ill to poor folk.

But will ye tell me, master Caesar,
Sure *great folk's* life's a life o' pleasure?
Nae cauld nor hunger e'er can steer them,   no cold, touch
The vera thought o't need na fear them.   very, not

CAESAR

Lord, man, were ye but whyles whare I am,   whiles, where
The *Gentles*, ye wad ne'er envy them!   would

It's true, they need na starve or sweat,   not
Thro' Winter's cauld, or Simmer's heat;   cold, summer's
They've nae sair-work to craze their banes,   no sore work, bones
An' fill *auld-age* wi' grips an' granes: old-age, gripes & groans
But *human bodies* are sic fools,   such
For a' their Colledges an' Schools,
That when nae *real* ills perplex them,   no
They *mak* enow themsels to vex them;
An' ay the less they hae to sturt them,   always, have, fret
In like proportion, less will hurt them.

A countra fellow at the pleugh,   country, plough
His *acre's* till'd, he's right eneugh;   well enough
A countra girl at her wheel,   country
Her *dizzen's* done, she's unco weel;   dozen's, very well
But Gentlemen, an' Ladies warst,

Wi' ev'n down *want o' wark* they're curst: work

They loiter, lounging, lank an' lazy;

Tho' deil-haet ails them, yet uneasy: nothing

Their days insipid, dull an' tasteless;

Their nights unquiet, lang an' restless.   long

An' ev'n their sports, their balls an' races,

Their galloping thro' public places,

There's sic parade, sic pomp an' art,   such

The joy can scarcely reach the heart.

The *Men* cast out in *party-matches*,   compete

Then sowther a' in deep debauches;   patch up

Ae night they're mad wi' drink an' whoring,   one

Niest day their life is past enduring.   next

The *Ladies* arm-in-arm in clusters,

As great an' gracious a' as sisters;   all

But hear their *absent thoughts* o' ither,

They're a' run deils an' jads thegither.   downright, together

Whyles, owre the wee bit cup an' platie,   whiles, over, plate

They sip the *scandal-potion* pretty;

Or lee-lang nights, wi' crabbet leuks   live-long, bad tempered looks

Pore owre the devil's *pictur'd beuks*;   over, books

Stake on a chance a farmer's stackyard,

An' cheat like onie *unhang'd blackguard*.   any, villain

There's some exceptions, man an' woman;
But this is Gentry's life in common.

By this, the sun was out o' sight,
An' darker gloamin brought the night;   fading twilight
The *bum-clock* humm'd wi' lazy drone;   beetle
The kye stood rowtin i' the loan;   cattle, lowing, field

When up they gat, an' shook their lugs,   got, ears
Rejoic'd they were na *men*, but *dogs*;   not
An' each took aff his several way,   went his different
Resolv'd to meet some ither day.   other

To a Louse
On Seeing One on a Lady's Bonnet at Church

Ha! whare ye gaun, ye crowlan ferlie! — *where, going, crawling wonder*

Your impudence protects you sairly: — *very well*

I canna say but ye strunt rarely — *cannot, strut confidently*

    Owre *gauze* and *lace*, — *over*

Tho' faith, I fear ye dine but sparely — *eat little*

    On sic a place. — *such*

Ye ugly, creepan, blastet wonner, — *blasted wonder*

Detested, shunn'd by saunt an' sinner, — *saint*

How daur ye set your fit upon her — — *dare, foot*

    Sae fine a *Lady*! — *so*

Gae somewhere else and seek your dinner — *go*

    On some poor body.

Swith, in some beggar's haffet squattle: — *away!, temples, squat*

There ye may creep, and sprawl, and sprattle, — *scramble*

Wi' ither kindred, jumping cattle, — *other*

    In shoals and nations;

Whare *horn* nor *bane* ne'er daur unsettle — *where, bone, dare*

    Your thick plantations.

Now haud you there, ye're out o' sight,   hold
Below the fatt'rels, snug an' tight,   ribbon-ends
Na, faith ye yet! ye'll no be right,   no, confound you
      Till ye've got on it,
The vera tapmost, tow'ring height   very / topmost
      O' *Miss's bonnet*.   hat

My sooth! right bauld ye set your nose out,   bold
As plump an' grey as onie grozet: any / gooseberry
O for some rank, mercurial rozet,   mercury / pasted rosin
      Or fell, red smeddum,   deadly / powder
I'd gie ye sic a hearty dose o't,   give
      Wad dress your droddum!   would, / backside

I wad na been surpris'd to spy   would not
You on an auld wife's *flainen toy*;   old flannel / cap
Or aiblins some bit duddie boy,   perhaps, / small ragged
      On's *wylecoat*;   flannel vest
But Miss's fine *Lunardi*, fye!   balloon-shaped hat
      How daur ye do't?   dare

O *Jenny*, dinna toss your head,   do not
An' set your beauties a' abroad!   abroad/on view
Ye little ken what cursèd speed   know / damned
      The blastie's makin!   thing's

Thae *winks* an' *finger-ends*, I dread,
    Are notice takin!

O wad some Pow'r the giftie gie us
To *see oursels as ithers see us*!
It wad frae monie a blunder free us,
    An' foolish notion:
What airs in dress an' gait wad lea'e us,
    An' ev'n Devotion!

---

they – who
see and
print

would, gift
give

others
would from
many

appearance,
would leave

To a Mouse

On Turning her up in her Nest with the Plough,
November 1785

Wee, sleekit, cowrin, tim'rous *beastie*,   small, sleek

O, what a panic's in thy breastie!   breast

Thou need na start awa sae hasty not,   away, so hasty,

         Wi' bickering brattle!   scurry

I wad be laith to rin an' chase thee,   would, loth, run

         Wi' murdering *pattle*!   a wooden plough-scraper

I'm truly sorry Man's dominion

Has broken Nature's social union,

An' justifies that ill opinion

         Which makes thee startle

At me, thy poor, earth-born companion

         An' *fellow mortal*!

I doubt na, whyles, but thou may thieve;   not, sometimes

What then? poor beastie, thou maun live!   must

A *daimen icker* in a *thrave*   one ear of corn in 24 sheaves

         'S a sma' request;

I'll get a blessin wi' the lave,   remainder

         An' never miss't!

Thy wee-bit *housie*, too, in ruin! — small, house/nest

Its silly wa's the win's are strewin! — walls, winds

An' naething, now, to big a new ane, — nothing, build, new one

    O' foggage green! — thick winter grass

An' bleak *December's win's* ensuin, — winds

    Baith snell an' keen! — both bitter, biting cold

Thou saw the fields laid bare an' waste,

An' weary *Winter* comin fast,

An' cozie here, beneath the blast, — cosy

    Thou thought to dwell,

Till crash! the cruel *coulter* past — plough blade

    Out thro' thy cell.

That wee bit heap o' leaves an' stibble, — small, stubble

Has cost thee monie a weary nibble! — many

Now thou's turned out, for a' thy trouble,

    But house or hald, — without, holding

To thole the Winter's *sleety dribble*, — endure, drizzle

    An' *cranreuch* cauld! — hoar-frost cold

But Mousie, thou art no thy lane, — not alone

In proving *foresight* may be vain:

The best-laid schemes o' *Mice* an' *Men*

    Gang aft agley, — go often wrong

An' lea'e us nought but grief an' pain, — leave

    For promis'd joy!

Still thou art blest, compared wi' me!
The *present* only toucheth thee:
But Och! I backward cast my e'e,
     On prospects drear!
An' *forward*, tho' I canna *see*,   cannot
     I *guess* an' *fear*!

Address to the Deil

O Prince! O Chief of many thronèd pow'rs!
That led th' embattl'd seraphim to war.

                 Milton

O Thou! whatever title suit thee —
Auld Hornie, Satan, Nick, or Clootie — _{old, cloven-hoofed}
Wha in yon cavern grim an' sootie, _{who, filled with soot}
       Clos'd under hatches,
Spairges about the brunstane cootie, _{splashes, brimstone dish}
         To scaud poor wretches! _{scald}

Hear me, *auld Hangie,* for a wee, _{old hangman, while}
An' let poor *damnèd bodies* be;
I'm sure sma' pleasure it can gie, _{give}
       Ev'n to a *deil,* _{devil}
To skelp an' scaud poor dogs like me _{hit/slap, scald}
         An' hear us squeel!

Great is thy pow'r an' great thy fame;

Far kend, an' noted is thy name; known

An' tho' yon *lowan heugh's* thy hame, moaning,
hollow, home

      Thou travels far;

An' faith! thou's neither lag, nor lame, backward

      Nor blate nor scaur. bashful,
afraid

Whyles, ranging like a roarin lion, sometimes

For prey, a' holes an' corners tryin;

Whyles, on the strong-wing'd Tempest flyin,

      Tirlan the *Kirks*; stripping –
attacking

Whyles, in the human bosom pryin,

      Unseen thou lurks.

I've heard my rev'rend *Graunie* say, grannie

In lanely glens ye like to stray; lonely

Or, where auld ruin'd castles grey old

      Nod to the moon,

Ye fright the nightly wand'rer's way

      Wi' eldritch croon. unearthly
eerie moan

When twilight did my *Graunie* summon, grannie

To say her pray'rs, douce, honest woman! sober/
prudent

Aft yont the dyke she's heard you bumman, away
beyond

      Wi' eerie drone;

Or, rustlin, thro' the boortries coman,

      Wi' heavy groan.

alder trees
coming

Ae dreary, windy, winter night,

The stars shot down wi' sklentan light,

Wi' you mysel, I gat a fright:

      Ayont the lough,

Ye, like a *rash-buss*, stood in sight,

      Wi' waving sugh:

one

slanting

got
beyond,
loch
bunch of
rushes

moan

The cudgel in my nieve did shake,

Each bristl'd hair stood like a stake;

When wi' an eldritch, stoor *quaick*, *quaick*,

      Amang the springs,

Awa ye squatter'd like a *drake*,

      On whistling wings.

fist

unearthly harsh,
duck quack

among
away, a noisy
take-off

Let *Warlocks* grim, an' wither'd *Hags*,

Tell how wi' you, on ragweed nags,

They skim the muirs an' dizzy crags,

      Wi' wicked speed;

And in kirk-yards renew their leagues,

      Owre howket dead.

ragwort
moors, high
peaks

over those
raised from
the grave

Thence, countra wives, wi' toil an' pain,   country

May plunge an' plunge the *kirn* in vain;   churn

For Och! the yellow treasure's taen   taken

       By witching skill;

An' dawtit, twal-pint *Hawkie's* gaen   petted, 12-pint
       As yell's the Bill.   cow has gone

                             dry, bull

Thence, mystic knots mak great abuse

On *Young-Guidmen*, fond, keen an' croose;   husbands,
                                                              over confident

When the best *warklum* i' the house,   work-tool,
                                                              penis

       By cantraip wit,   magic/evil

Is instant made no worth a louse,

       Just at the bit.   stopped before
                                                              ejaculation

When thowes dissolve the snawy hoord,   thaws, snowy
                                                              hoard

An' float the jinglin icy boord,   water's
                                                              surface

Then, *Water-kelpies* haunt the foord,   imaginary
                                                              water-spirits,
                                                              ford

       By your direction,

An' nighted Trav'llers are allur'd

       To their destruction.

An' aft your moss-traversing *Spunkies*   often, bog-,
                                                              demons

Decoy the wight that late an' drunk is: fellow

The bleezan, curst, mischievous monkies
      Delude his eyes,
Till in some miry slough he sunk   is, dirty hole
      Ne'er mair to rise.   more

When MASONS' mystic *word* an' *grip*
In storms an' tempests raise you up,
Some cock or cat your rage maun stop,   shall
      Or, strange to tell!
The *youngest Brother* ye wad whip   would
      Aff straught to *Hell*.   off straight

Lang syne in *Eden's* bonie yard,   long ago, bony garden
When youthfu' lovers first were pair'd,
An' all the Soul of Love they shar'd,
      The raptur'd hour,
Sweet on the fragrant flow'ry swaird,   grassy edge
      In shady bow'r:

Then you, ye auld, snick-drawing dog!   old, noisy door opener
Ye cam to Paradise incog,   came, disguised
An' play'd on man a cursed brogue   trick
      (Black be your fa'!),   fall
An' gied the infant warld a shog,   gave, world, shake
      'Maist ruin'd a'.   almost

D'ye mind that day when in a bizz

flurry/
bustle

Wi' reeket duds, an' reestet gizz,

smoky clothes,
scorched wig

Ye did present your smoutie phiz

obscene/
ugly face

    'Mang better folk;

An' sklented on the *man of Uzz*

squinted at
Job

    Your spitefu' joke?

An' how ye gat him i' your thrall,

got, spell

An' brak him out o' house an' hal',

broke

While scabs an' blotches did him gall,

    Wi' bitter claw;

An' lows'd his ill-tongu'd wicked *Scawl* —

slackened,
scolding wife

    Was warst ava?

worst of all

But a' your doings to rehearse,

Your wily snares an' fechtin fierce,

fighting

Sin' that day MICHAEL did you pierce

    Down to this time,

Wad ding a *Lallan* tongue, or *Erse*,

would, beat,
Lowland Scots,
Irish

    In Prose or Rhyme.

An' now, auld *Cloots*, I ken ye're thinkan,

old, know

A certain Bardie's rantin, drinkin,

Some luckless hour will send him linkan,

hurrying

    To your black pit;

Hell

But, faith! he'll turn a corner jinkin,   dodging
      An' cheat you yet.

But fare-you-weel, auld *Nickie-ben*!   old
O wad ye tak a thought an' men'!   would, mend
Ye aiblins might — I dinna ken —   perhaps, do not know
      Still hae a *stake*:   have
I'm wae to think upo' yon den,   sad
      Ev'n for your sake.

Address to a Haggis

Fair fa' your honest, sonsie face,   *good luck to, cheerful*
Great Chieftain o' the Puddin-race!
Aboon them a' ye tak your place,   *above*
    Painch, tripe, or thairm: *paunch, guts*
Weel are ye wordy of a *grace*   *well*
    As lang's my arm.   *long as*

The groaning trencher there ye fill,
Your hurdies like a distant hill,   *buttocks*
Your *pin* wad help to mend a mill   *skewer, would*
    In time o' need,
While thro' your pores the dews distil
    Like amber bead.

His knife see Rustic-labour dight,   *wipe*
An' cut ye up wi' ready slight,   *skill*
Trenching your gushing entrails bright,
    Like onie ditch;   *any*
And then, O what a glorious sight,
    Warm-reekin, rich!   *-steaming*

Then, horn for horn, they stretch an' strive:

Deil tak the hindmost, on they drive,

Till a' their weel-swall'd kytes belyve

    Are bent like drums;

Then auld Guidman, maist like to rive,

    Bethankit hums.

> eating with a
> horn-spoon
> devil take
> the *leftovers*
> well-swollen
> stomachs
> eventually
>
> old goodman,
> most, burst

Is there that owre his French *ragout*,

Or *olio* that wad staw a sow,

Or *fricassee* wad mak her spew

    Wi' perfect sconner,

Looks down wi' sneering, scornfu' view

    On sic a dinner?

> over
> would, fill
> up/bloat
> would make,
> throw up
>
> disgust
>
> such

Poor devil! see him owre his trash,

As feckless as a wither'd rash,

His spindle shank a guid whip-lash,

    His nieve a nit;

Thro' bluidy flood or field to dash,

    O how unfit!

> over
>
> feeble, rush
> thin leg,
> good
>
> fist, nut
>
> bloody

But mark the Rustic, *haggis-fed*,

The trembling earth resounds his tread,

> country
> man

Clap in his walie nieve a blade,   place, firm
                                     fist
    He'll make it whissle;   whistle/cutting
                                     through air
An' legs, an' arms, an' heads will sned   cut off
    Like taps o' thrissle.   tops of
                                     thistle

Ye Pow'rs wha mak mankind your care,   who make
And dish them out their bill o' fare,
Auld Scotland wants nae skinking ware,   old, no
                                     watery
    That jaups in luggies;   splashes in
                                     bowls
But, if ye wish her gratefu' prayer,
    Gie her a *Haggis*!   give

Holy Willie's Prayer

And send the Godly in a pet to pray.

Alexander Pope

O Thou that in the Heavens does dwell!
Wha, as it pleases best Thysel,   *who, thyself*
Sends ane to Heaven an' ten to Hell,   *one*
     A' for Thy glory!   *all*
And no for ony guid or ill   *any good*
     They've done before Thee. —

I bless and praise Thy matchless might,
When thousands Thou hast left in night,
That I am here before Thy sight,
     For gifts an' grace,
A burning and a shining light
     To a' this place. —

What was I, or my generation,
That I should get sic exaltation?   *such*

I, wha deserv'd most just damnation,   who
      For broken laws
Sax thousand years ere my creation,   six
      Thro' Adam's cause!

When from my mither's womb I fell,   mother's
Thou might hae plung'd me deep in hell,   have
To gnash my gooms, and weep, and wail,   gums
      In burning lakes,
Whare damned devils roar and yell   where
      Chain'd to their stakes. —

Yet I am here, a chosen sample,
To show Thy grace is great and ample:
I'm here a pillar o' Thy temple
      Strong as a rock,
A guide, a ruler and example
      To a' Thy flock. —

O Lord thou kens what zeal I bear,   knows
When drinkers drink, and swearers swear,
And singin' there, and dancin' here,
      Wi' great an' sma';   small
For I am keepet by Thy fear,   kept
      Free frae them a'. —   from, all

But yet — O Lord — confess I must —
At times I'm fash'd wi' fleshly lust;   troubled
And sometimes too, in warldly trust   worldly
      Vile Self gets in;
But Thou remembers we are dust,
      Defiled wi' sin. —

O Lord — yestreen — Thou kens —   last night, knows
           wi' Meg —
Thy pardon I sincerely beg!
O may't ne'er be a living plague,
      To my dishonour!
An' I'll ne'er lift a lawless leg
      Again upon her. —

Besides, I farther maun avow,   must
Wi' Leezie's lass, three times — I trow —
But, Lord, that Friday I was fou   full/drunk
      When I cam near her;   came
Or else, Thou kens, Thy servant true   knows
      Wad never steer her. —   would, meddle with

Maybe Thou lets this fleshly thorn
Buffet Thy servant e'en and morn,   evening
Lest he owre proud and high should turn,   over
      That he's sae gifted;   so

If sae, Thy han' maun e'en be borne

> Untill Thou lift it. —

so, hand
must

Lord, bless Thy chosen in this place,
For here Thou has a chosen race:
But God, confound their stubborn face,

> An' blast their name,

Wha bring Thy elders to disgrace

> An' open shame. —

who

Lord mind Gaun Hamilton's deserts!
He drinks, and swears, an' plays at cartes,
Yet has sae monie takin arts

> Wi' Great and Sma',

Frae God's ain priest the people's hearts

> He steals awa. —

Gavin
cards
so many
popular
small
from, own
away

And when we chasten'd him therefore,
Thou kens how he bred sic a splore,
And set the warld in a roar

> O' laughin at us:

Curse Thou his basket and his store,

> Kail an' potatoes. —

knows,
such, row
world
cabbage/
greens

Lord, hear my earnest cry and prayer
Against that Presbytry of Ayr!
Thy strong right hand, Lord, mak it bare
     Upon their heads!
Lord visit them, and dinna spare,   do not
     For their misdeeds!

O Lord my God, that glib-tongu'd Aiken!   loose-
My vera heart and flesh are quakin   very
To think how I sat, sweating, shaking,
     An' pish'd wi' dread,   wet myself
While Auld wi' hingin lip an' sneaking   hanging, sneering
     And hid his head!

Lord, in Thy day o' vengeance try him!
Lord visit him wha did employ him!   who
And pass not in Thy mercy by them,
     Nor hear their prayer;
But for Thy people's sake destroy them,
     An' dinna spare!   do not

But Lord, remember me and mine
Wi' mercies temporal and divine!
That I for grace an' gear may shine,
     Excell'd by nane!   none
And a' the glory shall be Thine!
     AMEN! AMEN!

Tam o' Shanter: A Tale

Of Brownyis and of Bogillis full is this Buke.
                                    Gawin Douglas

When chapman billies leave the street, *pedlar / friends*
And drouthy neebors, neebors meet, *thirsty / neighbours*
As market-days are wearing late,
An' folk begin to tak the gate; *road/go home*
While we sit bousing at the nappy, *drinking, ale*
And getting fou and unco happy, *full/drunk, mighty*
We think na on the lang Scots miles, *not, long*
The mosses, waters, slaps, and styles, *bogs, pools, stiles*
That lie between us and our hame, *home*
Whare sits our sulky sullen dame, *where*
Gathering her brows like gathering storm,
Nursing her wrath to keep it warm.

This truth fand honest *Tam o' Shanter*, *found*
As he frae Ayr ae night did canter, *from, one*
(Auld Ayr, wham ne'er a town surpasses *who/that*
For honest men and bonie lasses).

O *Tam!* had'st thou but been sae wise,   so

As taen thy ain wife *Kate's* advice!   taken, own

She tauld thee weel thou was a skellum,   told, well, rogue

A blethering, blustering, drunken blellum;   chattering, babbling, idle talker

That frae November till October,   from

Ae market-day thou was nae sober;   one, not

That ilka melder, wi' the miller,   every meal, grinding

Thou sat as lang as thou had siller;   long, money

That ev'ry naig was ca'd a shoe on,   horse, shod

The smith and thee gat roaring fou on;   got, full/drunk

That at the Lord's house, even on Sunday,

Thou drank wi' Kirkton Jean till Monday.

She prophesied that late or soon,

Thou would be found deep drown'd in Doon;

Or catch'd wi' warlocks in the mirk,   wizards, dark

By *Alloway's* auld, haunted kirk.   old

Ah, gentle dames! it gars me greet,   makes, weep

To think how mony counsels sweet,   many

How mony lengthen'd, sage advices,   many

The husband frae the wife despises!   from

But to our tale: — Ae market-night,   one

Tam had got planted unco right;   mighty

Fast by an ingle, bleezing finely, — fire, blazing
Wi' reaming swats, that drank divinely — foaming ale
And at his elbow, Souter *Johnny,* — cobbler
His ancient, trusty, drouthy crony; — drinking pal
Tam lo'ed him like a very brither — — loved, brother
They had been fou for weeks thegither! — full/drunk, together
The night drave on wi' sangs and clatter — drove, songs, chat

And ay the ale was growing better:
The landlady and *Tam* grew gracious,
Wi' favours, secret, sweet and precious:
The Souter tauld his queerest stories; — cobbler told
The landlord's laugh was ready chorus:
The storm without might rair and rustle, — roar
Tam did na mind the storm a whistle. — not

Care, mad to see a man sae happy, — so
E'en drown'd himsel amang the nappy: — among, ale
As bees flee hame wi' lades o' treasure, — fly home, loads
The minutes wing'd their way wi' pleasure:
Kings may be blest, but *Tam* was glorious,
O'er a' the ills o' life victorious!

But pleasures are like poppies spread,
You seize the flower, its bloom is shed;

Or like the snow falls in the river,
A moment white — then melts for ever;
Or like the borealis race,
That flit ere you can point their place;
Or like the rainbow's lovely form
Evanishing amid the storm. —
Nae man can tether time or tide;   *no, hold/ control*
The hour approaches *Tam* maun ride;   *must*
That hour, o' night's black arch the key-stane,   *-stone*
That dreary hour he mounts his beast in;
And sic a night he taks the road in,   *such, takes*
As ne'er poor sinner was abroad in.

    The wind blew as 'twad blawn its last;   *it would have blown*
The rattling showers rose on the blast;
The speedy gleams the darkness swallow'd;
Loud, deep, and lang, the thunder bellow'd: *long*
That night, a child might understand,
The Deil had business on his hand.   *devil*

    Weel mounted on his gray mare, *Meg* —   *well*
A better never lifted leg —
Tam skelpit on thro' dub and mire,   *rode fast, puddle*
Despising wind, and rain, and fire;
Whyles holding fast his guid blue bonnet;   *good*

Whyles crooning o'er some auld Scots sonnet; *muttering,*
old

Whyles glow'ring round wi' prudent cares, *looking*
with fear

Lest bogles catch him unawares: *bogies*

Kirk-Alloway was drawing nigh,

Whare ghaists and houlets nightly cry. — *where*
ghosts, owls

　　By this time he was cross the ford, *burn*

Whare in the snaw the chapman smoor'd; *where, snow,*
pedlar, smothered

And past the birks and meikle stane, *birches, big*
stone

Whare drunken *Charlie* brak's neck-bane; *where, broke*
his, -bone

And thro' the whins, and by the cairn, *gorse*
bushes

Whare hunters fand the murder'd bairn; *where,*
found, child

And near the thorn, aboon the well, *above*

Whare *Mungo's* mither hang'd hersel. — *where,*
mother

Before him *Doon* pours all his floods;

The doubling storm roars thro' the woods;

The lightnings flash from pole to pole;

Near and more near the thunders roll:

When, glimmering thro' the groaning trees,

Kirk-Alloway seem'd in a bleeze; *blaze/lit up*
every chink
in the wall

Thro' ilka bore the beams were glancing;

And loud resounded mirth and dancing.

　　Inspiring bold *John Barleycorn!*

What dangers thou canst make us scorn!

Wi' tippenny, we fear nae evil;

Wi' usquabae, we'll face the Devil! —

The swats sae ream'd in *Tammie's* noddle,

Fair play, he car'd na deils a boddle.

But *Maggie* stood, right sair astonish'd,

Till, by the heel and hand admonish'd,

She ventur'd forward on the light;

And, vow! *Tam* saw an unco sight!

Warlocks and witches in a dance;

Nae cotillion brent new frae *France*,

But hornpipes, jigs, strathspeys, and reels,

Put life and mettle in their heels.

A winnock-bunker in the east,

There sat auld Nick, in shape o' beast;

A tousie tyke, black, grim, and large,

To gie them music was his charge:

He screw'd the pipes and gart them skirl,

Till roof and rafters a' did dirl. —

Coffins stood round, like open presses,

That shaw'd the dead in their last dresses;

And by some devilish cantraip sleight,

Each in its cauld hand held a light. —

By which heroic *Tam* was able

To note upon the haly table,

A murderer's banes, in gibbet-airns;

Marginal glosses (right column):

cheap two-penny ale, no

whisky
small beers, so, mind
cared not a farthing

sore
spurred and slapped

strange/
wondrous

wizards
no, brand
new from

window
recess

old

shaggy dog

give

made, blare

ring/shake

showed

magic trick

cold

holy

bones, -irons

Twa span-lang, wee, unchristen'd bairns; *two, -long, babies*

A thief new-cutted frae a rape, *from, rope*

Wi' his last gasp his gab did gape; *mouth, gasp*

Five tomahawks wi' blude red-rusted; *axes, blood*

Five scymitars wi' murder crusted;

A garter, which a babe had strangled;

A knife, a father's throat had mangled,

Whom his ain son o' life bereft, *own*

The grey-hairs yet stack to the heft; *stuck, handle*

[Three Layers' tongues, turned inside out,

Wi' lies seamed like a beggar's clout;

Three Priests' hearts, rotten black as muck,

Lay stinking, vile, in every neuk]. *corner*

As *Tammie* glowr'd, amaz'd, and curious, *stared*

The mirth and fun grew fast and furious:

The piper loud and louder blew;

The dancers quick and quicker flew;

They reel'd, they set, they cross'd, they cleekit, *clasped one another*

Till ilka carlin swat and reekit, *every witch, sweated, steamed*

And coost her duddies to the wark, *cast off clothes, work*

And linket at it in her sark! *set to it, shirt*

Now *Tam*, O *Tam*! had thae been queans,   they, girls
A' plump and strapping in their teens,
Their sarks, instead o' creeshie flannen,   shirts, greasy
                                                 flannel
Been snaw-white seventeen hunder linen!   snow-, fine
                                                 threaded linen
Thir breeks o' mine, my only pair,   these
                                                 breeches
That ance were plush, o' guid blue hair,   once, good
I wad hae gi'en them off my hurdies,   would have given,
                                                 backside
For ae blink o' the bonie burdies!   one, bony
                                                 lasses

But wither'd beldams, auld and droll,   hags, old
Rigwoodie hags wad spean a foal,   tough, would,
                                                 abort
Louping and flinging on a crummock,   jumping,
                                                 cudgel
I wonder did na turn thy stomach.   not

But *Tam* kend what was what fu' brawlie,   knew, full
                                                 well
There was ae winsome wench and wawlie,   one comely,
                                                 choice
That night enlisted in the core,
(Lang after kend on *Carrick* shore;   long, known
For mony a beast to dead she shot,   many
An' perish'd mony a bonie boat,   many, bony
And shook baith meikle corn and bear,   both much,
                                                 barley
And kept the country-side in fear).

Her cutty-sark, o' Paisley harn   short shirt,
                                                 coarse cloth
That while a lassie she had worn,

In longitude tho' sorely scanty, — revealing

It was her best, and she was vauntie. — proud of it

Ah! little kend thy reverend grannie, — knew

That sark she coft for her wee Nannie, — shirt, bought

Wi' twa pund Scots ('twas a' her riches), — two pounds

Wad ever grac'd a dance of witches! — would

But here my Muse her wing maun cour; — must fold/curb

Sic flights are far beyond her pow'r; — such

To sing how Nannie lap and flang, — leaped, kicked

(A souple jad she was, and strang), — supple lass, strong

And how *Tam* stood like ane bewitch'd, — one

And thought his very een enrich'd; — eyes

Even Satan glowr'd, and fidg'd fu' fain, — stared, fidgeted excitedly

And hotch'd and blew wi' might and main: — jerked

Till first ae caper, syne anither, — one, then another

Tam tint his reason a' thegither, — lost, together

And roars out, 'Weel done, Cutty-sark!' — well

And in an instant all was dark:

And scarcely had he *Maggie* rallied,

When out the hellish legion sallied.

As bees bizz out wi' angry fyke, — buzz, fret

When plundering herds assail their byke; — hive

As open pussie's mortal foes, — a hare's

When, pop! she starts before their nose;
As eager runs the market-crowd,
When 'Catch the thief!' resounds aloud;
So *Maggie* runs, the witches follow,
Wi' mony an eldritch skriech and hollow.   *many, unearthly screech*

Ah, *Tam*! ah, *Tam*! thou'll get thy fairin'!   *reward/due*
In hell they'll roast thee like a herrin'!
In vain thy *Kate* awaits thy comin'!
Kate soon will be a woefu' woman!
Now, do thy speedy utmost, Meg,
And win the key-stane of the brig;   *key-stone, bridge*
There, at them thou thy tail may toss,
A running stream they dare na cross.   *not*
But ere the key-stane she could make,   *key-stone*
The fient a tail she had to shake!   *little of*
For Nannie, far before the rest,
Hard upon noble *Maggie* prest,   *pressed*
And flew at *Tam* wi' furious ettle;   *aim*
But little wist she Maggie's mettle —   *was*
Ae spring brought off her master hale,   *one, whole*
But left behind her ain grey tail: *own*
The carlin claught her by the rump,   *old witch caught*
And left poor *Maggie* scarce a stump.

Now, wha this tale o' truth shall read, who
Ilk man and mother's son take heed: each
Whene'er to drink you are inclin'd,
Or cutty-sarks run in your mind, short shirts/ skirts
Think! ye may buy the joys o'er dear —
Remember *Tam o' Shanter's* mare.

A Man's a Man for a' That

Is there, for honest Poverty
    That hings his head, an' a' that;   *hangs*
The coward-slave, we pass him by,
    We dare be poor for a' that!
For a' that, an' a' that,
    Our toils obscure, an' a' that,
The rank is but the guinea's stamp,
    The Man's the gowd for a' that.   *gold*

What though on hamely fare we dine,   *homely foods*
    Wear hoddin grey, an' a' that?   *coarse woollen cloth*
Gie fools their silks, and knaves their wine,   *give*
    A Man's a Man for a' that.
For a' that, an' a' that,
    Their tinsel show, an' a' that;
The honest man, tho' e'er sae poor,   *so*
    Is king o' men for a' that.

Ye see yon birkie ca'd a lord,   *fellow*
    Wha struts, an' stares, an' a' that,   *called*
Tho' hundreds worship at his word,
    He's but a coof for a' that.   *fool/lout*
For a' that, an' a' that,
    His ribband, star, an' a' that,
The man o' independent mind,
    He looks an' laughs at a' that.

A prince can mak a belted knight,
    A marquis, duke, an' a' that!
But an honest man's aboon his might —   *above*
    Guid faith, he mauna fa' that!   *good, must not be like*
For a' that, an' a' that,
    Their dignities, an' a' that,
The pith o' Sense an' pride o' Worth
    Are higher rank than a' that.

Then let us pray that come it may,
    As come it will for a' that,
That Sense and Worth o'er a' the earth
    Shall bear the gree an' a' that.   *win the day*
For a' that, an' a' that,
    It's comin yet for a' that,
That Man to Man the warld o'er   *world*
    Shall brithers be for a' that.   *brothers*

Such a Parcel of Rogues in a Nation

Fareweel to a' our Scottish fame,   farewell
    Fareweel our ancient glory;
Fareweel even to the Scottish name,
    Sae famed in martial story!   so
Now Sark rins o'er the Solway sands,   runs
    And Tweed rins to the ocean,   runs
To mark whare England's province stands,   where
    Such a parcel of rogues in a nation!

What force or guile could not subdue,
    Thro' many warlike ages,
Is wrought now by a coward few,
    For hireling traitors' wages.
The English steel we could disdain,
    Secure in valour's station;
But English gold has been our bane,
    Such a parcel of rogues in a nation!

O would, or I had seen the day
    That Treason thus could sell us,
My auld grey head had lien in clay,   old, lain
    Wi' BRUCE and loyal WALLACE!
But pith and power, till my last hour,
    I'll mak this declaration;
We're bought and sold for English gold,
    Such a parcel of rogues in a nation!

Westlin Winds

Now westlin winds and slaught'ring guns
 Bring Autumn's pleasant weather;
The moorcock springs on whirring wings
 Amang the blooming heather:
Now waving grain, wide o'er the plain,
 Delights the weary Farmer;
The moon shines bright, as I rove at night
 To muse upon my Charmer.

The Paitrick lo'es the fruitfu' fells,
 The Plover lo'es the mountains;
The Woodcock haunts the lanely dells,
 The soaring Hern the fountains;
Thro' lofty groves the Cushat roves,
 The path o' man to shun it;
The hazel bush o'erhangs the Thrush,
 The spreading thorn the Linnet.

from the west

partridge loves

lonely

heron wood pigeon

Thus ev'ry kind their pleasure find,
    The savage and the tender;
Some social join, and leagues combine,
    Some solitary wander:
Avaunt, away! the cruel sway,
    Tyrannic man's dominion!
The Sportsman's joy, the murd'ring cry,
    The flutt'ring, gory pinion!

But, PEGGY dear, the ev'ning's clear,
    Thick flies the skimming swallow,
The sky is blue, the fields in view
    All fading-green and yellow:
Come let us stray our gladsome way,
    And view the charms o' Nature;
The rustling corn, the fruited thorn,
    And ilka happy creature.   *every*

We'll gently walk, and sweetly talk,
    While the silent moon shines clearly;
I'll clasp thy waist, and, fondly prest,
    Swear how I lo'e thee dearly: *love*
Not vernal show'rs to budding flow'rs,
    Not Autumn to the Farmer,
So dear can be as thou to me,
    My fair, my lovely Charmer!

A Red, Red Rose

O my Luve's like a red, red rose,
    That's newly sprung in June;
O my Luve's like the melodie
    That's sweetly play'd in tune. —

As fair art thou, my bonie lass,
    So deep in luve am I;
And I will luve thee still, my Dear,
    Till a' the seas gang dry. —   go

Till a' the seas gang dry, my Dear,   go
    And the rocks melt wi' the sun:
I will luve thee still, my Dear,
    While the sands o' life shall run. —

And fare thee weel, my only Luve!   well
    And fare thee weel, a while!
And I will come again, my Luve,
    Tho' it were ten thousand mile!

Mary Morison

O Mary, at thy window be,
    It is the wish'd, the trysted hour;
Those smiles and glances let me see,
    That make the miser's treasure poor:
How blythely wad I bide the stoure, *would, abide, dust/struggle*
    A weary slave frae sun to sun; *from*
Could I the rich reward secure,
    The lovely Mary Morison!

Yestreen when to the trembling string *yesterday evening*
    The dance gaed thro' the lighted ha', *went, hall*
To thee my fancy took its wing,
    I sat, but neither heard or saw:
Though this was fair, and that was braw, *fine/good looking*
    And yon the toast of a' the town, *an other, all*
I sigh'd, and said amang them a', *among, all*
    'Ye are na Mary Morison.' *you are not*

O Mary, canst thou wreck his peace,
    Wha for thy sake wad gladly die!   who, would
Or canst thou break that heart of his,
    Whase only faut is loving thee!   fault
If love for love thou wilt na gie,   will not give
    At least be pity to me shown;
A thought ungentle canna be   cannot be
    The thought o' Mary Morison.

Ae Fond Kiss

Ae fond kiss, and then we sever;   one
Ae fareweel, and then forever!   one
Deep in heart-wrung tears I'll pledge thee,
Warring sighs and groans I'll wage thee. —

Who shall say that Fortune grieves him,
While the star of hope she leaves him:
Me, nae cheerfu' twinkle lights me;   no
Dark despair around benights me. —

I'll ne'er blame my partial fancy:
Naething could resist my Nancy: nothing
But to see her, was to love her;
Love but her, and love for ever. —

Had we never lov'd sae kindly,   so
Had we never lov'd sae blindly!   so
Never met — or never parted,
We had ne'er been broken-hearted. —

61

Fare-thee-weel, thou first and fairest!   -well
Fare-thee-weel, thou best and dearest!
Thine be ilka joy and treasure,   each/every
Peace, Enjoyment, Love and Pleasure! —

Ae fond kiss, and then we sever!
Ae fareweel, Alas, for ever!
Deep in heart-wrung tears I'll pledge thee,
Warring sighs and groans I'll wage thee. —

Auld Lang Syne

Should auld acquaintance be forgot   old
  And never brought to mind?
Should auld acquaintance be forgot,
  And auld lang syne!   long ago

Chorus
For auld lang syne, my jo,   friend
  For auld lang syne,
We'll tak a cup o' kindness yet
  For auld lang syne.

And surely ye'll be your pint stowp!   pay for
  And surely I'll be mine!
And we'll tak a cup o' kindness yet,
  For auld lang syne.
      For auld lang syne, &c.

We twa hae run about the braes,   two,
  And pou'd the gowans fine;   hillsides
                                       pulled,
                                       daisies

63

But we've wander'd mony a weary fitt, many, foot
    Sin auld lang syne.
        For auld lang syne, &c.

We twa hae paidl'd in the burn, two have paddled
    Frae morning sun till dine; from
But seas between us braid hae roar'd, broad have
    Sin auld lang syne.
        For auld lang syne, &c.

And there's a hand, my trusty fiere! companion
    And gie's a hand o' thine! give me
And we'll tak a right gude-willie-waught, good-will drink
    For auld lang syne!
        For auld lang syne, &c.

CANONGATE CLASSICS

Books listed in alphabetical order by author:

The Bruce John Barbour, AAM Duncan (ed.)
   ISBN 0 86241 681 7 £9.99
The Land of the Leal James Barke
   ISBN 0 86241 142 4 £7.99
Farewell Miss Julie Logan: A JM Barrie Omnibus
   (The Little White Bird, The Twelve-Pound Look,
   Farewell Miss Julie Logan)
   JM Barrie
   ISBN 0 84195 003 3 £7.99
The Scottish Enlightenment: An Anthology A Broadie (ed.)
   ISBN 0 86241 738 4 £10.99
The House with the Green Shutters
   George Douglas Brown
   ISBN 0 86241 549 7 £5.99
Magnus George Mackay Brown
   ISBN 0 86241 814 3 £5.99
The Leithen Stories (The Power-House, John Macnab,
   The Dancing Floor, Sick Heart River) John Buchan
   ISBN 0 86241 995 6 £8.99
The Watcher by the Threshold: Shorter Scottish Fiction
   John Buchan
   ISBN 0 86241 682 5 £7.99
Witchwood John Buchan
   ISBN 0 86241 202 1 £6.99

The Life of Robert Burns Catherine Carswell
  ISBN 0 86241 292 7 £6.99
Lying Awake Catherine Carswell
  ISBN 0 86241 683 3 £5.99
Open the Door! Catherine Carswell
  ISBN 0 86241 644 2 £5.99
The Triumph Tree: Scotland's Earliest Poetry 550–1350
  Thomas Owen Clancy (ed.)
  ISBN 0 86241 787 2 £9.99
Twentieth-Century Scottish Drama: An Anthology
  Craig/Stevenson (eds)
  ISBN 0 86241 979 4 £12.99
Two Worlds David Daiches
  ISBN 0 86241 704 X £5.99
The Complete Brigadier Gerard Arthur Conan Doyle
  ISBN 0 86241 534 9 £6.99
A Glasgow Trilogy George Friel
  ISBN 086241 885 2 £9.99
Dance of the Apprentices Edward Gaitens
  ISBN 0 86241 297 8 £7.99
Ringan Gilhaize John Galt
  ISBN 0 86241 552 7 £6.99
The Member and the Radical John Galt
  ISBN 0 86241 642 6 £5.99
Memoirs of a Highland Lady vols I & II
  Elizabeth Grant of Rothiemurchus
  ISBN 0 86241 396 6 £8.99

The Highland Lady in Ireland
   Elizabeth Grant of Rothiemurchus
   ISBN 0 86241 361 3 £8.99
A Scots Quair (Sunset Song, Cloud Howe, Grey Granite)
   Lewis Grassic Gibbon
   ISBN 0 86241 532 2 £6.99
Smeddum: A Lewis Grassic Gibbon Anthology
   Valentina Bold (ed.)
   ISBN 0 86241 965 4 £11.99
Sunset Song Lewis Grassic Gibbon
   ISBN 0 86241 179 3 £4.99
Unlikely Stories, Mostly Alasdair Gray
   ISBN 0 86241 737 6 £6.99
Highland River Neil M. Gunn
   ISBN 0 86241 358 3 £5.99
The Key of the Chest Neil M. Gunn
   ISBN 0 86241 770 8 £6.99
The Serpent Neil M. Gunn
   ISBN 0 86241 728 7 £6.99
Sun Circle Neil M. Gunn
   ISBN 0 86241 587 X £6.99
The Well at the World's End Neil M. Gunn
   ISBN 0 86241 645 0 £5.99
Gillespie J. MacDougall Hay
   ISBN 0 86241 427 X £6.99
The Private Memoirs and Confessions of a Justified Sinner
   James Hogg
   ISBN 0 86241 340 0 £5.99

The Three Perils of Man James Hogg
ISBN 0 86241 646 9 £8.99
Flemington & Tales from Angus Violet Jacob
ISBN 0 86241 784 8 £8.99
Fergus Lamont Robin Jenkins
ISBN 0 86241 310 9 £6.99
Just Duffy Robin Jenkins
ISBN 0 86241 551 9 £5.99
The Changeling Robin Jenkins
ISBN 0 86241 228 5 £5.99
Journey to the Hebrides (A Journey to the Western Isles
of Scotland, The Journal of a Tour to the Hebrides)
Samuel Johnson & James Boswell
ISBN 0 86241 588 8 £6.99
Household Ghosts: A James Kennaway Omnibus
(Tunes of Glory, Household Ghosts, Silence)
James Kennaway
ISBN 1 84195 125 0 £7.99
Wisdom, Madness and Folly RD Laing
ISBN 0 86241 831 3 £5.99
The Haunted Woman David Lindsay
ISBN 0 86241 162 9 £6.99
A Voyage to Arcturus David Lindsay
ISBN 0 86241 377 X £6.99
Ane Satyre of the Thrie Estaitis Sir David Lindsay
ISBN 0 86241 191 2 £4.99
The Dark of Summer Eric Linklater
ISBN 0 86241 894 1 £5.99

Magnus Merriman Eric Linklater
  ISBN 0 86241 313 3 £6.99
Private Angelo Eric Linklater
  ISBN 0 86241 376 1 £5.99
Scottish Ballads Emily Lyle (ed.)
  ISBN 0 86241 477 6 £5.99
Nua-Bhardachd Ghaidhlig/Modern Scottish Gaelic Poems
  Donald MacAulay (ed.)
  ISBN 0 86241 494 6 £4.99
The Early Life of James McBey James McBey
  ISBN 0 86241 445 8 £5.99
Three Scottish Poets MacCaig, Morgan, Lochhead
  ISBN 0 86241 400 8 £6.99
And the Cock Crew Fionn MacColla
  ISBN 0 86241 536 5 £4.99
The Devil and the Giro: Two Centuries of Scottish Stories
  Carl MacDougall (ed.)
  ISBN 0 86241 359 1 £9.99
St Kilda: Island on the Edge of the World Charles Maclean
  ISBN 0 86241 388 5 £6.99
Linmill Stories Robert McLellan
  ISBN 0 86241 282 X £6.99
Homeward Journey John MacNair Reid
  ISBN 0 86241 178 5 £3.95
The Silver Bough F. Marian McNeill
  ISBN 0 86241 231 5 £6.99
Wild Harbour Ian Macpherson
  ISBN 0 86241 234 X £6.99

A Childhood in Scotland Christian Miller
   ISBN 0 86241 230 7 £4.99
The Blood of the Martyrs Naomi Mitchison
   ISBN 0 86241 192 0 £8.99
The Corn King and the Spring Queen Naomi Mitchison
   ISBN 0 86241 287 0 £9.99
The Gowk Storm Nancy Brysson Morrison
   ISBN 0 86241 222 6 £4.99
An Autobiography Edwin Muir
   ISBN 0 86241 423 7 £6.99
The Wilderness Journeys (The Story of My Boyhood and
   Youth, A Thousand Mile Walk to the Gulf, My First
   Summer in the Sierra, Travels in Alaska, Stickeen)
   John Muir
   ISBN 0 86241 586 1 £9.99
Imagined Selves: (Imagined Corners, Mrs Ritchie, Mrs
   Grundy in Scotland, Women: An Inquiry, Women in
   Scotland) Willa Muir
   ISBN 0 86241 605 1 £8.99
A Beleaguered City: Tales of the Seen and Unseen
   Margaret Oliphant
   ISBN 1 84195 060 2 £7.99
A Twelvemonth and a Day Christopher Rush
   ISBN 0 86241 439 3 £6.99
The End of an Old Song J.D. Scott
   ISBN 0 86241 311 7 £4.95
The Journal of Sir Walter Scott WEK Anderson (ed.)
   ISBN 0 86241 828 3 £12.99

The Grampian Quartet (The Quarry Wood, The Weatherhouse, A Pass in the Grampians, The Living Mountain) Nan Shepherd
ISBN 0 86241 589 6 £9.99

Consider the Lilies Iain Crichton Smith
ISBN 0 86241 415 6 £4.99

Listen to the Voice: Selected Stories Iain Crichton Smith
ISBN 0 86241 434 2 £7.99

Diaries of a Dying Man William Soutar
ISBN 0 86241 347 8 £6.99

Markheim, Jekyll and the Merry Men: Shorter Scottish Fiction Robert Louis Stevenson
ISBN 0 86241 555 1 £6.99

Tales of Adventure (Black Arrow, Treasure Island, 'The Sire de Malétroit's Door' and other stories) Robert Louis Stevenson
ISBN 0 86241 687 6 £7.99

Tales of the South Seas (Island Landfalls, The Ebb-tide, The Wrecker) Robert Louis Stevenson
ISBN 0 86241 643 4 £7.99

The Scottish Novels (Kidnapped, Catriona, The Master of Ballantrae, Weir of Hermiston) Robert Louis Stevenson
ISBN 0 86241 533 0 £6.99

The Makars: The Poems of Henryson, Dunbar and Douglas JA Tasioulas (ed.)
ISBN 0 86241 820 8 £9.99

Divided Loyalties Janet Teissier du Cros
ISBN 0 86241 375 3 £8.99

The Bad Sister: An Emma Tennant Omnibus (The Bad
  Sister, Two Women of London, Wild Nights)
  Emma Tennant
  ISBN 1 84195 053 X £7.99
The People of the Sea David Thomson
  ISBN 1 84195 107 2 £6.99
The City of Dreadful Night James Thomson
  ISBN 0 86241 449 0 £5.99
Black Lamb and Grey Falcon Rebecca West
  ISBN 0 86241 428 8 £12.99
The King and the Lamp: Scottish Traveller Tales
  Duncan and Linda Williamson
  ISBN 1 84195 063 7 £7.99